Addition Clue Words

Some clue words tell you to add. These clue words are: **in all**, **all together**, **sum**, and **total**. There are six steps to follow when solving all story problems.

1. Read the problem carefully.
2. Look for clue words and underline them.
3. Decide what you must do.
4. Write the number sentence.
5. Solve the problem.
6. Write a complete sentence that includes the answer.

Sara saw **23** butterflies when she was walking in the field. When she stopped to rest, she saw **10** grasshoppers. How many insects did she see <u>all together</u>?

The number sentence:

$$\begin{array}{r} 23 \\ + 10 \\ \hline 33 \end{array}$$

The answer:

Sara saw **33** insects all together.

Underline the word or words that give you the clue to add. Then use the six steps to solve the story problem.

1. While hiking in the woods, Calvin picked up **34** rocks. He then spotted **12** new rocks and picked them up also. What is the total number of rocks that Calvin found?

2. Yesterday Jamie saw **14** birds in her yard. Today she saw **39** birds in her yard. How many birds did she see in all?

Addition Story Problems

Underline the word or words that give you the clue to add.
Solve the problem. Remember to follow the six steps.

1. Stephanie has **25** dolls in her collection.
   She receives **11** more for her birthday.
   What is the total number of dolls
   Stephanie has in her collection?

2. Dalton has **31** baseball cards. His dad
   gives him **22** more. How many baseball
   cards does he have in all?

3. Andy counted **64** dandelions. Beth
   counted **26** violets. What is the sum
   of the flowers they counted?

4. Adam found **91** small twigs and **29** larger
   twigs for the campfire. How many twigs
   did he find all together?

5. In her week of camping, Krista saw
   15 chipmunks run for the safety of their
   homes. She also saw **15** squirrels climb
   into the trees. How many animals
   did Krista see in all?

6. Alesha caught **52** fish. Yumiko caught
   39 fish. What is the total number of fish
   they caught?

Subtraction Clue Words

Some clue words tell you to subtract. These clue words are: **how many more**, **how many are left**, and **difference**. The same six steps you used for addition can also be used for subtraction problems.

1. Read the problem carefully.
2. Look for clue words and underline them.
3. Decide what you must do.
4. Write the number sentence.
5. Solve the problem.
6. Write a complete sentence that includes the answer.

Steve played **12** games with his baseball team. His team will be playing **57** games this season. How many more games will Steve need to play to complete the season?

The number sentence:

$$\begin{array}{r} 57 \\ -\ 12 \\ \hline 45 \end{array}$$

The answer:

Steve needs to play **45** more games to complete the season.

Underline the word or words that give you the clue to subtract. Then use the six steps to solve the story problems.

1. Chelsea threw the ball **29** feet. Meagan threw the ball **27** feet. What was the difference in feet between their throws?

2. Yesterday John kicked the soccer ball **68** times during the game. Today he kicked the ball **49** times. How many more times did he kick the ball yesterday?

Subtraction Story Problems

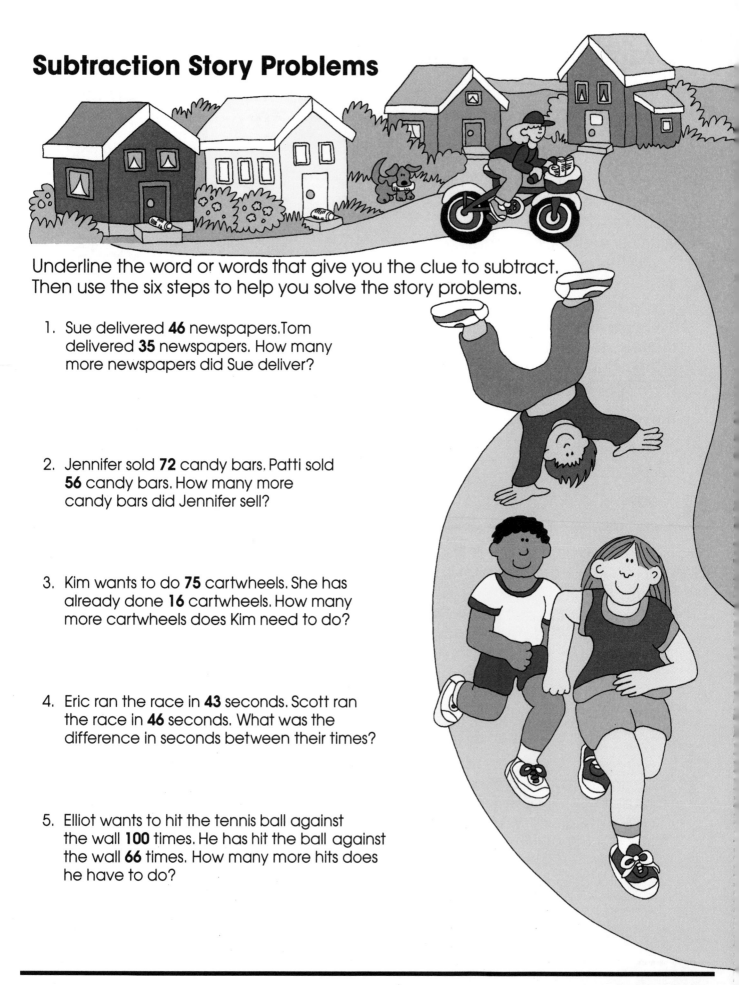

Underline the word or words that give you the clue to subtract. Then use the six steps to help you solve the story problems.

1. Sue delivered **46** newspapers. Tom delivered **35** newspapers. How many more newspapers did Sue deliver?

2. Jennifer sold **72** candy bars. Patti sold **56** candy bars. How many more candy bars did Jennifer sell?

3. Kim wants to do **75** cartwheels. She has already done **16** cartwheels. How many more cartwheels does Kim need to do?

4. Eric ran the race in **43** seconds. Scott ran the race in **46** seconds. What was the difference in seconds between their times?

5. Elliot wants to hit the tennis ball against the wall **100** times. He has hit the ball against the wall **66** times. How many more hits does he have to do?

Add or Subtract

On this page you will need to decide whether to add or subtract. Remember the six steps.

1. Read the problem carefully.
2. Look for clue words and underline them.
3. Decide what you must do.
4. Write the number sentence.
5. Solve the problem.
6. Write a complete sentence that includes the answer.

There are **178** sixth grade students and **106** fifth grade students. <u>How many more</u> sixth grade students are there?

What to do:

subtract

The answer:

There are **72** more sixth grade students.

Decide what to do. Then solve the story problems.

1. In our school there are **328** girls and **297** boys. How many children are there in our school all together?

   What to do: _____   The answer: _____

2. The class painted **10** pictures on Monday and **13** pictures on Tuesday. How many more pictures did they paint on Tuesday?

   What to do: _____   The answer: _____

3. Jessica brought **45** pennies to school and Sam brought **25** pennies to school. How many pennies did they bring in all?

   What to do: _____   The answer: _____

4. Miss Bracken had **160** pieces of chalk. She broke **73** of them. How many pieces were left unbroken?

   What to do: _____   The answer: _____

Addition and Subtraction Problems

Write the number sentences. Solve the problems.

1. There were **16** spotted butterflies in the field. They were joined by **18** plain butterflies. What is the sum of the butterflies in the field?

2. There are **15** spiders on the porch. If **10** of those spiders leave the porch, how many spiders will be left?

3. There are **98** grasshoppers in the grass. There are also **65** beetles in the grass. How many more grasshoppers are there?

4. There were **120** brown ants and **92** black ants marching down the ant hill. How many more brown ants were there?

5. There are **127** big flies buzzing around the pond. Also buzzing are **112** little flies. How many flies are there all together?

6. There are **25** bees and **13** hornets flying near the bush. How many insects are there in all?

Addition and Subtraction Story Problems

Addition and Subtraction Problems

When adding money, keep the decimal points in line.

Jacob bought a pencil for **$.92** He also bought an eraser for **$.37**. How much money did he spend all together?

The number sentence:

$$\begin{array}{r} \$\ .92 \\ +\ \$\ .37 \\ \hline \$1.29 \end{array}$$

The answer: He spent **$1.29** all together.

Write the number sentences. Solve the problems.

1. Molly bought a box of cat food for **$1.64**. She then went to the candy store and bought some gum for **$.35**. How much money did she spend in all?

2. Mandi bought a book that cost **$5.00**. Her friend Justin bought a used book that cost **$.25**. How much more did Mandi spend?

3. Jaric saw a bottle of shampoo that cost **$1.72**. He also saw conditioner that cost **$1.18**. If he purchased both items, what would the sum be?

4. At a garage sale, Nancy bought a baseball card that cost **$3.01**. She also purchased a ring for **$.45**. How much money did she spend in all?

5. Lauren bought some beads for **$2.60**. She later bought some string for **$.55**. How much more money did she spend on the beads?

Addition and Subtraction Problems

Write the number sentences. Solve the problems.

1. The band marched **65** minutes in the morning and **45** minutes in the afternoon. How many minutes did the band march all together?

2. The band has **25** tubas and **19** trombones. How many more tubas does the band have?

3. The band went on a field trip. It traveled **275** miles going and **280** miles returning. How many miles did the band travel in all?

4. There are **29** flutes in the band and **20** drums. What is the difference in number between these instruments?

5. There are **125** people in the band. There are only **65** uniforms. How many more uniforms are needed?

6. Jill knows how to play **26** marching songs. Jack knows how to play **32**. How many more songs does Jack know?

Drawing Multiplication Story Problems

Use a graph to help you to organize information in a story problem and keep your information accurate. Here is an example:

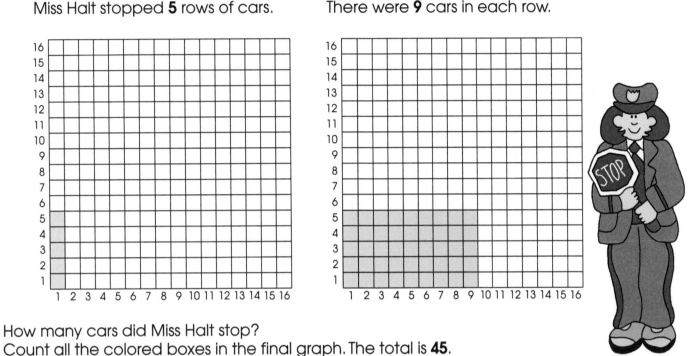

Miss Halt stopped **5** rows of cars.

There were **9** cars in each row.

How many cars did Miss Halt stop?
Count all the colored boxes in the final graph. The total is **45**.

Read and solve each problem using the method shown above.

1. Miss Halt helps about **15** people across the street each week.

2. Suppose Miss Halt gave **12** tickets in a day.

How many people does she help in **4** weeks? _____

If she did this for **6** days, how many tickets would she give? _____

3. Miss Halt practiced directing traffic. She practiced for **7** hours a day. She practiced for **11** days.

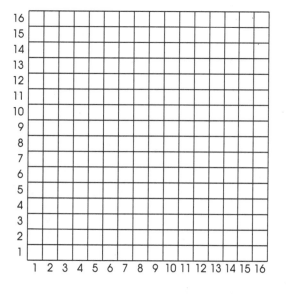

How many hours did she practice?

_____

4. Miss Halt has **10** boxes. In each box she has **10** whistles.

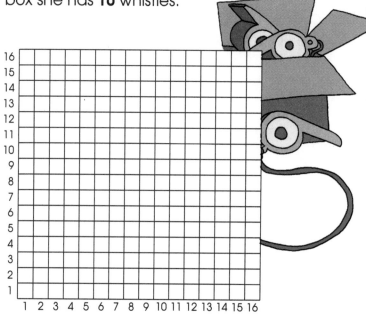

How many whistles does she have?

_____

5. Miss Halt blew her whistle **12** times in one day. She blew it that many times each day for **3** days.

How many times did she blow her whistle?

_____

6. Miss Halt gave directions to **14** people. Each person asked **5** questions.

How many questions were asked?

_____

Drawing Multiplication Story Problems

Drawing Division Story Problems

Here is another example of how a picture can help you solve a story problem:

Carl has **3** toolboxes. He needs to divide **15** hammers equally among all his toolboxes.

First draw **3** toolboxes. Then, beginning with the first box, draw one dot in each box. Each dot will represent one hammer. Repeat until all **15** hammers are drawn.

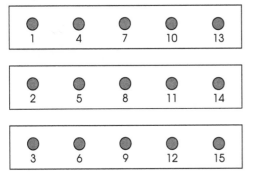

How many hammers will he put in each box?
Count the number of dots that were drawn in one box. The answer will be **5**.

Read and solve each problem using the drawing method shown above.

1. There are **4** construction workers. There are a total of **32** nails. How many nails does each worker get in order to have an equal number of nails?

2. There are **8** construction workers. They have **56** screwdrivers. How many screwdrivers will each worker get in order to have an equal number of screwdrivers?

3. There are **5** trucks. There are **35** pieces of wood. How many pieces of wood would be placed into each truck so that each truck has an equal number of wood pieces?

4. There are **7** toolboxes. There are **49** saws. How many saws will be in each box in order to have an even number in each box?

5. There were **8** people with drills. There were **48** holes drilled into the wall. Each person drilled an equal number of holes. How many holes did each person drill?

6. There were **6** toolboxes. There were **42** wrenches. Each toolbox contained an equal number of wrenches. How many wrenches were in each box?

Drawing Division Story Problems

Multiplication Clue Words

Some clue words tell you to multiply. These clue words are **how many** and **how much**. Remember that multiplication is a quicker form of addition. Use the six steps to help you solve the story problems.

There were **15** people ready to begin the race. Each person had **2** water bottles at the finish line. How many water bottles were there at the finish line?

The number sentence:

$$\begin{array}{r} 15 \\ \times\ \ 2 \\ \hline 30 \end{array}$$

The answer:

There were **30** water bottles at the finish line.

Underline the clue words that tell you to multiply. Then solve the story problems.

1. There are **7** swimmers waiting for their finishing ribbons. Each swimmer will receive **3** ribbons. How many finishing ribbons are there all together?

2. Amy swam for **5** hours every day to train for the big race. She trained for **30** days. How many hours did she spend training?

3. There were **72** bikers at the start of the race. Each biker had **1** helmet. How many helmets were there?

Multiplication Story Problems

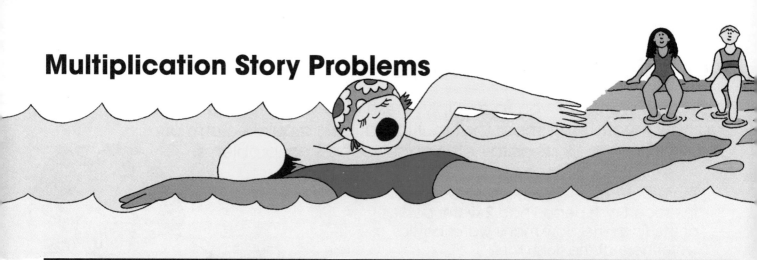

Underline the clue words that tell you to multiply. Then solve the story problems.

1. There were **16** golfers from each school at the tournament. **5** schools participated. How many golfers were there all together?

2. Dana drove his snowmobile **37** miles a day for **8** days. How many miles did he drive in all?

3. Curtis trained for **39** days to get ready for the race. He drank **8** glasses of water every day that he trained. How much water did Curtis drink throughout his training?

4. There were **8** rows of bikers. There were **6** bikers in each row. How many bikers were there all together?

5. There were **96** swimmers waiting to race. Each swimmer brought **4** friends to watch the race. How many friends were there at the race?

More Multiplication Story Problems

Write the number sentences. Then solve the story problems.

1. There were **57** skaters at the start of the race. Each skater had **2** knee pads. How many knee pads were there?

2. Keli practiced for **19** days to prepare for her dance recital. Every day she practiced for **3** hours. How many hours did she practice in all?

3. Daniel has **3** cases to hold his toy trucks. Each case holds **18** trucks. How many trucks can Daniel store in his cases?

4. Nadia's classroom has **12** rows of chairs. Each row has **5** chairs. How many chairs are in Nadia's classroom?

Division Clue Words

Some clue words mean to divide. These clue words are: **how many** and **each**. To solve each story problem use the six steps.

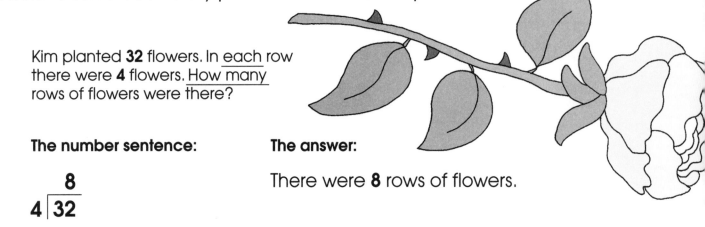

Kim planted **32** flowers. In <u>each</u> row there were **4** flowers. <u>How many</u> rows of flowers were there?

The number sentence:

$$4 \overline{\smash{)}32}^{\,8}$$

The answer:

There were **8** rows of flowers.

Underline the clue words that tell you to divide. Solve the problems.

1. Alesha planted **7** rows of carrots in her garden. Later, she pulled up the same number of carrots from each row. She counted **56** carrots. How many carrots did she pull from each row?

2. Scott and Brad had **48** flowers. They put **6** flowers in each vase. How many vases did they fill?

3. Caleb and John planted **30** rosebushes in **10** rows. Each row had the same number of bushes. How many rosebushes were in each row?

Division Story Problems

Underline the word or words that tell you to divide. Solve the problems.

1. Jory had **56** pieces of candy. If he put **8** pieces into each bag, how many bags did he have?

2. Jamal planted **20** rows of onions in his garden. He pulled an equal number of onions from each row. He counted **100** onions. How many onions did he pull from each row?

3. James was planting pine trees for his parents' tree farm. He planted **81** trees. There were **9** trees in each row. How many rows were there?

4. Margie has **45** plants in the tray she bought. The tray is divided into **9** rows How many plants are in each row?

5. George picked **63** apples from **7** trees. He picked an equal number of apples from each tree. How many apples did he pick from each tree?

Division Story Problems

More Division Story Problems

Write the number sentences. Then solve the story problems.

1. Katlin had **30** dolls. She divided them evenly
   among herself and **4** friends. How many dolls
   did each of the **5** girls have?

2. Jason swam **81** laps over a **9**-day period.
   If he swam the same distance every day,
   how many laps did he swim each day?

3. Dorry likes to send postcards to her friends. She
   mailed **24** postcards to **12** friends. Each
   friend received the same number of cards. How
   many postcards did each friend receive?

4. If a stamp costs **$.32**, how many stamps
   could you buy with **$12.80**?

Multiplication and Division Story Problems

Write the number sentences. Then solve the story problems.

1. Jamie bought **17** stamps. Andrew bought **3** times as many stamps. How many stamps did Andrew buy?

2. There are **40** letters in the mail bag. They are for **5** people. If each person gets the same number of letters, how many letters will each person get?

3. Miss James delivered **48** packets of letters. Each packet had **9** letters in it. How many letters did Miss James deliver?

4. Donna has pen pals in **15** countries. Suppose she has **3** pen pals in each country. How many pen pals does she have?

5. Mr. Koontz had **72** postcards. He put them in **9** equal piles. How many postcards were in each pile?

6. Miss James delivered **63** packages. She took **9** packages to each house. To how many houses did Miss James deliver packages?

Multiplication and Division Story Problems

Write the number sentences. Solve the problems.

1. The Smiths drove **55** miles an hour for **5** hours. How many miles did they drive?

2. Tim Smith collects postcards. He has **81** postcards. He keeps equal numbers of postcards in **9** envelopes. How many postcards are in each envelope?

3. Mrs. Smith took pictures of the trip. If she took **125** pictures a day for **7** days, how many pictures would she take?

4. Ann Smith saw bears on **9** mountains. Suppose each mountain had **32** bears on it. How many bears were there?

5. Mr. Smith packed **12** shirts. He packed them into **4** suitcases. If there were an equal number of shirts in each suitcase, how many shirts would be in each?

6. The Smiths rode on a cable car. There were **25** people waiting in line. Each cable cars holds **5** people. How many cable cars were needed to carry all the people?

Fractions

A **fraction** is a number that names a part of a whole.

$\dfrac{2}{3}$ — numerator
        — denominator

$\dfrac{2}{3}$ = **2** pieces out of **3** equal parts.

$\dfrac{2}{3}$ pieces colored
      pieces in all

$\dfrac{1}{3}$ $\dfrac{1}{3}$ $\dfrac{1}{3}$

$\dfrac{2}{3}$ pieces are triangles
      pieces in all

Read and solve each problem using the method shown above.

1.

How many pieces
are colored?

_____

How many pieces
are in the whole?

2.

How many pieces
are colored?

_____

How many pieces
are in the whole?

3.

How many pieces
are colored?

_____

How many pieces
are in the whole?

4.

How many pieces
are colored?

_____

How many pieces
are in the whole?

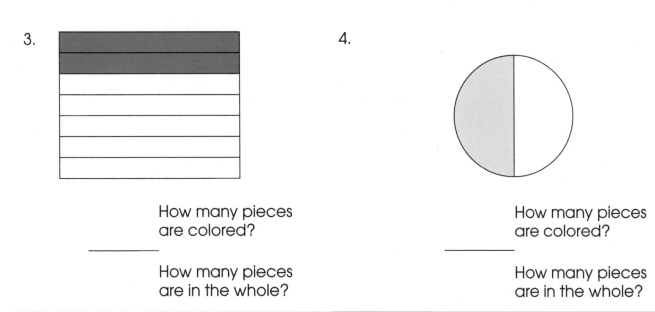

Adding and Subtracting Fractions

When you add or subtract fractions, you use only the top numbers (numerators). Below is an example:

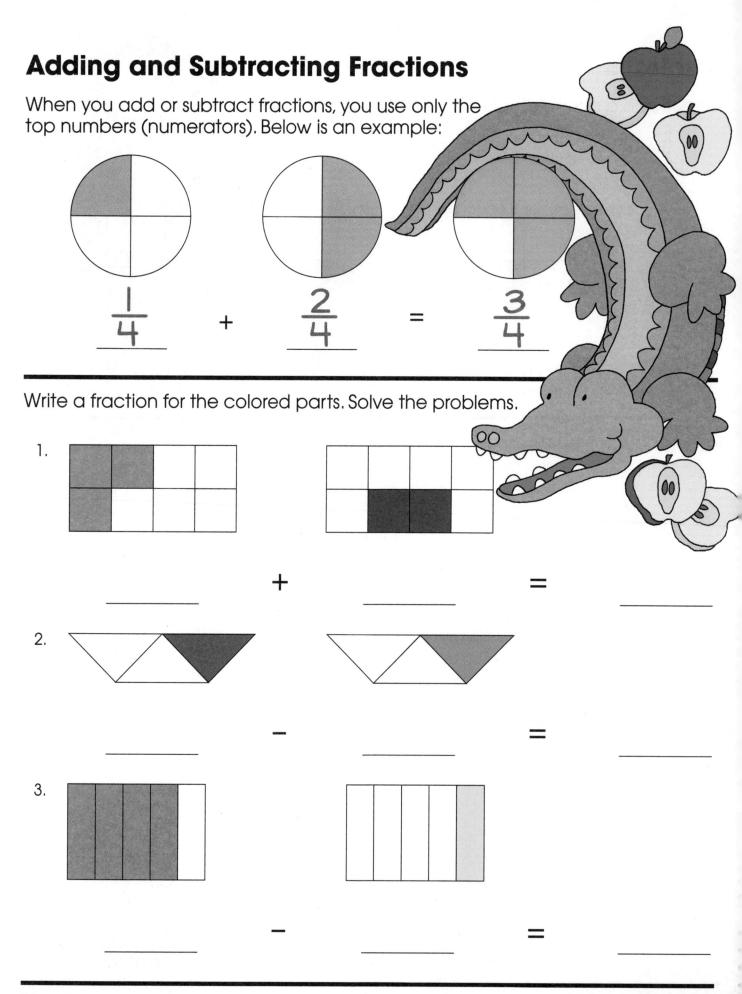

$$\frac{1}{4} \quad + \quad \frac{2}{4} \quad = \quad \frac{3}{4}$$

Write a fraction for the colored parts. Solve the problems.

1.

_____ + _____ = _____

2.

_____ − _____ = _____

3.

_____ − _____ = _____

Fractions in Story Problems

Sometimes you have fractions in story problems. Look for the clue words that tell you to add or subtract. Remember to add or subtract only the top number (numerator) of the fractions.

1. Read the problem carefully.
2. Look for clue words and underline them.
3. Decide what you must do.
4. Write the number sentence.
5. Solve the problem.
6. Write a complete sentence that includes the answer.

Mary planted **2/7** of the garden with corn and **3/7** with beans. How much of the garden did she use?

The number sentence:

$$\frac{2}{7} + \frac{3}{7} = \frac{5}{7}$$

The answer:

Mary used **5/7** of the garden.

Using the six steps, solve the story problems.

1. Wanda picked corn. She picked **8/9** of a bushel on Wednesday. She picked **5/9** of a bushel on Thursday. How much more did she pick on Wednesday than Thursday?

2. Kim dug **2/4** of the garden in the morning and **1/4** in the evening. How much of the garden did she dig all together?

3. Suzanne must plant **8/16** of the garden. She has planted **2/16** so far. How much more must she plant?

More Fractions in Story Problems

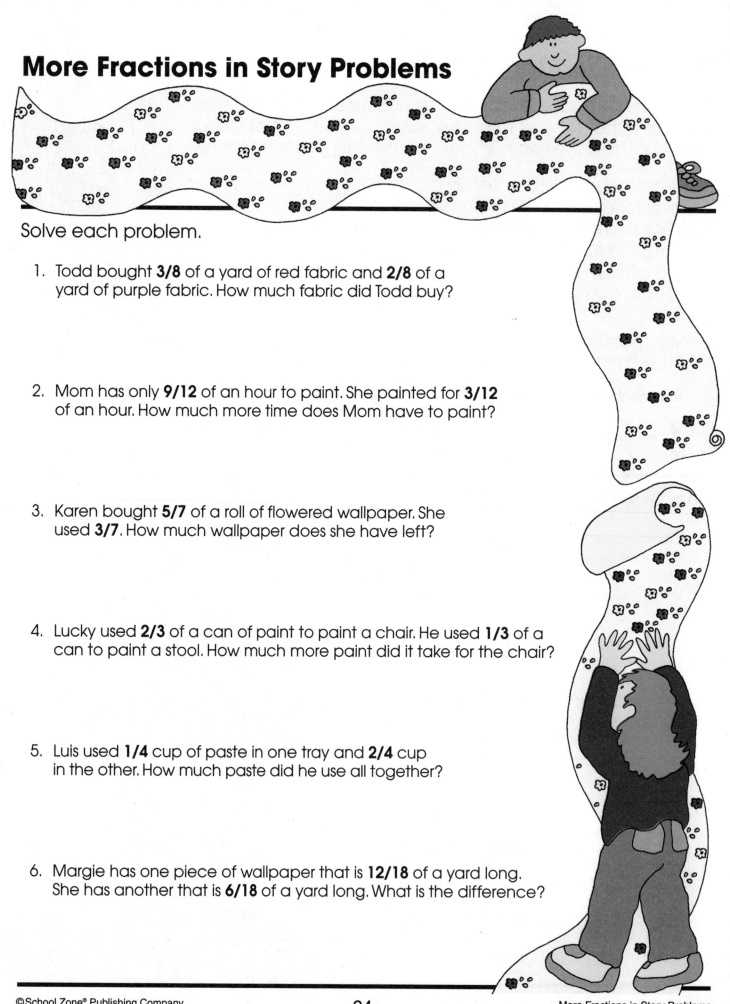

Solve each problem.

1. Todd bought **3/8** of a yard of red fabric and **2/8** of a yard of purple fabric. How much fabric did Todd buy?

2. Mom has only **9/12** of an hour to paint. She painted for **3/12** of an hour. How much more time does Mom have to paint?

3. Karen bought **5/7** of a roll of flowered wallpaper. She used **3/7**. How much wallpaper does she have left?

4. Lucky used **2/3** of a can of paint to paint a chair. He used **1/3** of a can to paint a stool. How much more paint did it take for the chair?

5. Luis used **1/4** cup of paste in one tray and **2/4** cup in the other. How much paste did he use all together?

6. Margie has one piece of wallpaper that is **12/18** of a yard long. She has another that is **6/18** of a yard long. What is the difference?

Logic Puzzles

These puzzles give you enough information to solve them, if you take some time to think. The logic puzzles on this and the next page have charts for you to record important information.

Patti, Mary, and Paul have different favorite foods of chicken, pizza, or spaghetti. Decide what food is each child's favorite using the information below.

Patti does not like chicken.

	Patti	Mary	Paul
Pizza			
Spaghetti			
Chicken	no		

Mary will not eat foods that have tomatoes in them. (Hint: If Mary does not eat foods with tomato, then she must like chicken.)

	Patti	Mary	Paul
Pizza		no	
Spaghetti		no	
Chicken	no	yes	

Paul likes a food that starts with the same letter as his name. (Hint: If Paul likes pizza, then spaghetti or chicken must not be his favorite.)

	Patti	Mary	Paul
Pizza		no	yes
Spaghetti		no	no
Chicken	no	yes	no

What is each child's favorite food?

Patti _____

Mary _____

Paul _____

Logic Puzzles

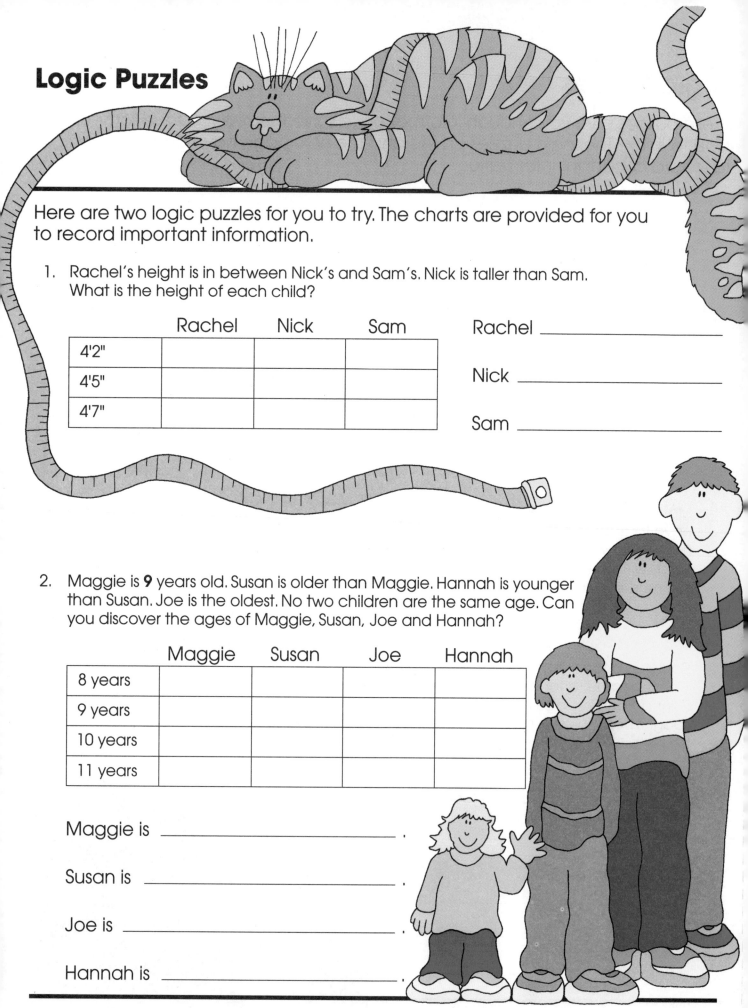

Here are two logic puzzles for you to try. The charts are provided for you to record important information.

1. Rachel's height is in between Nick's and Sam's. Nick is taller than Sam. What is the height of each child?

	Rachel	Nick	Sam
4'2"			
4'5"			
4'7"			

Rachel _____

Nick _____

Sam _____

2. Maggie is **9** years old. Susan is older than Maggie. Hannah is younger than Susan. Joe is the oldest. No two children are the same age. Can you discover the ages of Maggie, Susan, Joe and Hannah?

	Maggie	Susan	Joe	Hannah
8 years				
9 years				
10 years				
11 years				

Maggie is _____ .

Susan is _____ .

Joe is _____ .

Hannah is _____ .

Two-Step Problems

Sometimes you must use two steps to solve a problem. These problems are called two-step story problems.

Step 1:
$5.00 for a pair of shorts
+ $3.50 for a shirt
$8.50 total per outfit

There are **9** girls on the basketball team. Each girl needs a shirt and shorts for the games. A shirt costs **$3.50**. A pair of shorts cost **$5.00**. What is the total cost of all the outfits?

Step 2:
$8.50 per outfit
X   9 number of girls
$76.50 for 9 outfits

Step 1: Add to get the cost of one outfit.
Step 2: Multiply to get the cost of all the outfits.

The answer:

The total cost of all the outfits is **$76.50**.

Tell what the two steps are for each problem. Then solve the problem.

1. Angie has gym class **40** minutes a day. She has it **3** times a week. Nancy has gym class **90** minutes a week. How much more time does Angie spend in gym class?

2. Craig put **208** tennis balls into **4** wire baskets. He put the same number of balls in each basket. Then he took **3** baskets of balls outdoors. How many tennis balls did Craig take outdoors?

3. P.J. sold **4** rabbits for **$3.75** each and **1** rabbit for **$4.50**. How much money did he make all together?

4. Tim bought **6** tickets to the County Fair. Each ticket cost **$1.50**. How much change did he get from **$10.00**?

Venn Diagrams

A **Venn diagram** uses circles to represent sets and their relationships.

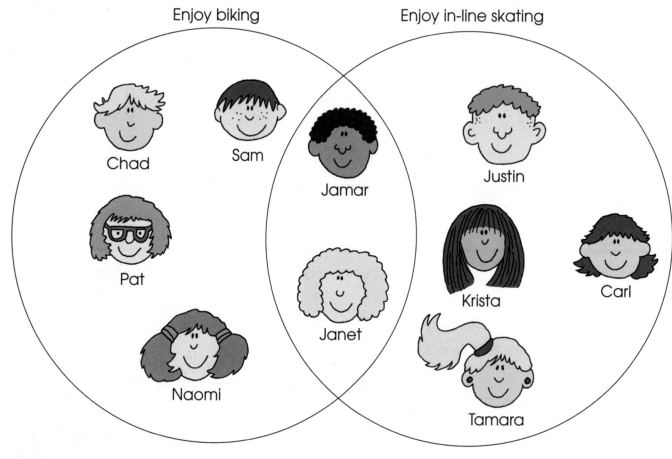

Ten children were surveyed to discover whether they enjoyed bicycling, in-line skating, or both. The Venn diagram above gives you all the information you need to answer the following questions. Hint: Where the circles overlap, the children are in both sets.

1. Which activity does Tamara enjoy? _____

2. Naomi and Sam enjoy the same activity. Which one is it? _____

3. How many children enjoy biking? _____

4. How many children enjoy in-line skating? _____

5. Who enjoys both biking and in-line skating? _____

6. How many children enjoy both biking and in-line skating? _____

Picture Graphs

A picture graph gives you information. Read it carefully. Make certain you understand what facts are presented.

Enrollment in Joy School

BOYS	👤	👤	👤	👤	👤	👤			
GIRLS	👤	👤	👤	👤	👤	👤	👤		

Each symbol 👤 stands for **20** students.

1. How many boys are in Joy School? __120 boys__ (**20 x 6 = 120**)

2. How many girls are in Joy School? __140 girls__ (**20 x 7 = 140**)

Read the graph carefully. Make certain you understand what facts are presented. Then answer the questions.

Days riding bikes to school

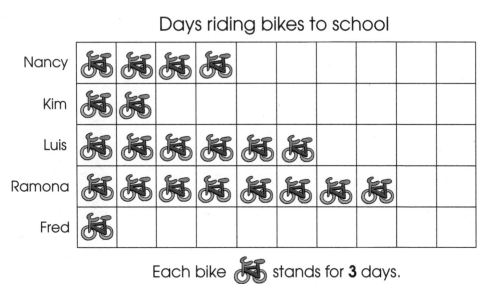

Nancy	🚲	🚲	🚲	🚲					
Kim	🚲	🚲							
Luis	🚲	🚲	🚲	🚲	🚲	🚲			
Ramona	🚲	🚲	🚲	🚲	🚲	🚲	🚲	🚲	
Fred	🚲								

Each bike 🚲 stands for **3** days.

1. Who rode to school the most days? _____

2. How many days did he or she ride to school? _____

3. How many days did Luis ride to school? _____

4. Nancy rode to school more days than Kim.
   How many more days did Nancy ride to school? _____

Bar Graphs

A bar graph gives you information. Read the graph carefully. Make sure you understand what facts are presented.

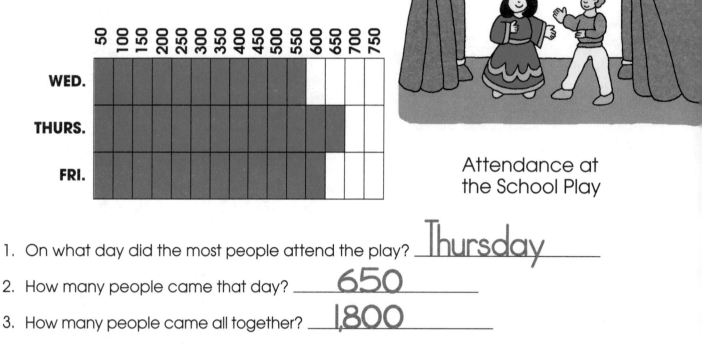

Attendance at the School Play

	50	100	150	200	250	300	350	400	450	500	550	600	650	700	750
WED.															
THURS.															
FRI.															

1. On what day did the most people attend the play? __Thursday__

2. How many people came that day? __650__

3. How many people came all together? __1,800__

Study the graph. Then answer the questions.

	10	20	30	40	50
Albert					
Jennifer					
Lucy					
Todd					
Shirley					

Tickets Sold to the School Play

1. Who sold the most tickets? _____

2. How many did Albert and Jennifer sell all together? _____

3. How many did Lucy and Todd sell in total? _____

4. Todd sold more tickets than Shirley.
   How many more tickets did Todd sell? _____

5. Shirley sold more tickets than Albert.
   How many more tickets did Shirley sell? _____

Answer Key

Page 1

1. Calvin found **46** rocks in total.
2. Jamie saw **53** birds in all.

Page 2

1. Stephanie has a total of **36** dolls in her collection.
2. Dalton has **53** baseball cards in all.
3. They counted a sum of **90** flowers.
4. Adam found **120** twigs all together.
5. Krista saw **30** animals in all.
6. They caught a total of **91** fish.

Page 3

1. The difference between their throws was **2** feet.
2. John kicked the ball **19** more times yesterday.

Page 4

1. Sue delivered **11** more newspapers than Tom.
2. Jennifer sold **16** more candy bars than Patti.
3. Kim has **59** cartwheels left to do.
4. The difference between their times was **3** seconds.
5. Elliot has to do **34** hits.

Page 5

1. add; There are **625** children in our school all together.
2. subtract; They painted **3** more pictures on Tuesday.
3. add; They brought **70** pennies in all.
4. subtract; There were **87** pieces of chalk left unbroken.

Page 6

1. The sum of butterflies in the field is **34**.
2. There will be **5** spiders left.
3. There are **33** more grasshoppers than beetles.
4. There were **28** more brown ants.
5. There are **239** flies all together.
6. There are **38** insects in all.

Page 7

1. She spent **$1.99** in all.
2. Mandi spent **$4.75** more than Justin.
3. The sum of both items would be **$2.90**.
4. She spent **$3.46** in all.
5. She spent **$2.05** more on the beads.

Page 8

1. The band marched **110** minutes all together.
2. The band has **6** more tubas than trombones.
3. The band traveled **555** miles in all.
4. The difference between them is **9**.
5. **60** more uniforms are needed.
6. Jack knows **6** more songs.

Pages 9 and 10

1. **60** people
2. **72** tickets
3. **77** hours
4. **100** whistles
5. **36** times
6. **70** questions

Pages 11 and 12

1. **8** nails
2. **7** screwdrivers
3. **7** pieces of wood
4. **7** saws
5. **6** holes
6. **7** wrenches

Page 13

1. There are **21** ribbons all together.
2. She spent **150** hours training.
3. There were **72** helmets.

Page 14

1. There were **80** golfers all together.
2. He drove **296** miles in all.
3. Curtis drank **312** glasses of water throughout his training.
4. There were **48** bikers all together.
5. There were **384** friends at the race.

Answer Key

Page 15
1. There were **114** knee pads.
2. She practiced **57** hours in all.
3. Daniel can store **54** trucks in his cases.
4. There are **60** chairs in Nadia's classroom.

Page 16
1. She pulled **8** carrots from each row.
2. They filled **8** vases.
3. There were **3** rosesbushes in each row.

Page 17
1. He had **7** bags.
2. He pulled **5** onions from each row.
3. There were **9** rows.
4. There are **5** plants in each row.
5. He picked **9** apples from each tree.

Page 18
1. Each girl had **6** dolls.
2. He swam **9** laps each day.
3. Each friend received **2** postcards.
4. You could buy **40** stamps.

Page 19
1. Andrew bought **51** stamps.
2. Each person will get **8** letters.
3. Miss James delivered **432** letters.
4. She has **45** pen pals.
5. There were **8** postcards in each pile.
6. Miss James delivered packages to **7** houses.

Page 20
1. They drove **275** miles.
2. There are **9** postcards in each envelope.
3. She would take **875** pictures.
4. There were **288** bears.
5. There would be **3** shirts in each suitcase.
6. **5** cable cars were needed.

Page 21
1. $\frac{1}{3}$
2. $\frac{3}{5}$
3. $\frac{2}{7}$
4. $\frac{1}{2}$

Page 22
1. $\frac{3}{8} + \frac{2}{8} = \frac{5}{8}$
2. $\frac{1}{3} - \frac{1}{3} = 0$
3. $\frac{4}{5} - \frac{1}{5} = \frac{3}{5}$

Page 23
1. She picked **3/9** (1/3) of a bushel more on Wednesday than Thursday.
2. She dug **3/4** of the garden all together.
3. She has **6/16** (3/8) of the garden more to plant.

Page 24
1. Todd bought **5/8** of a yard of fabric.
2. Mom has **6/12** (1/2) of an hour more to paint.
3. She has **2/7** of a roll of wallpaper left.
4. It took **1/3** of a can of paint more for the chair.
5. He used **3/4** of a cup of paste all together.
6. The difference is **6/18** (1/3) of a yard.

Page 25
spaghetti
chicken
pizza

Page 26
1. 4'5"
   4'7"
   4'2"
2. 9
   10
   11
   8

Page 27
1. Angie has gym class **30** minutes longer than Nancy.
2. Craig took **156** tennis balls outdoors.
3. He made **$19.50** all together.
4. He got **$1.00** in change from $10.00.

Page 28
1. in-line skating
2. biking
3. **6** children
4. **6** children
5. Jamar and Janet
6. **2** children

Page 29
1. Ramona
2. **24** days
3. **18** days
4. **6** days

Page 30
1. Todd
2. **30** tickets
3. **90** tickets
4. **20** tickets
5. **10** tickets

Comparing and Ordering Numbers

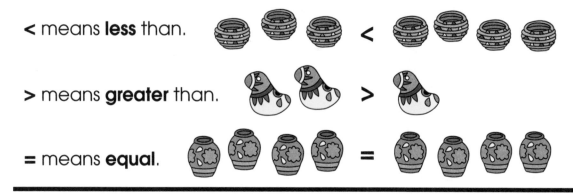

< means **less** than.

> means **greater** than.

= means **equal**.

Use one of the above signs to compare the numbers below.

1.	**687** _____ **593**	2. **254** _____ **221**	3. **8 x 8** _____ **6 x 10**
	5,213 _____ **8,436**	**3,333** _____ **3,491**	**20 – 6** _____ **2 x 7**
	7,549 _____ **9,264**	**9,054** _____ **9,268**	**10 + 9** _____ **5 x 5**

Put the numbers in order from the least to the greatest.

4. **149 822 324 287**

_____

5. **2,973 3,006 2,118 3,652**

_____

6. **4,431 2,840 4,931 2,821**

_____

Problem Solving

7. Three muchachas were racing. Juanita ran **135** yards, Maria ran **560** yards, and Lucia ran **310** yards. Order the names of the girls on the line from the least to the greatest distance.

_____

_____   _____   _____

Place Value

Mexico City's elevation is **7,579** feet above sea level.

7   **5**   **7**   **9**

thousands   hundreds   tens   ones

Write the correct number in each blank.

1. Mexico City has more than **350** neighborhood districts.

_____ _____ _____ _____

thousands   hundreds   tens   ones

2. The longest river, the Rio Bravo, is **1,880** miles.

_____ _____ _____ _____

thousands   hundreds   tens   ones

3. Mexico's Air Force has more than **5,500** people.

_____ _____ _____ _____

thousands   hundreds   tens   ones

Black skimmer

Write each number in standard form.

9,000 + 700 + 20 + 5 (expanded form)
9,725 (standard form)

4. **7,000 + 400 + 30 + 2**

_____

5. **6,000 + 300 + 40 + 1**

_____

6. **1,000 + 90 + 5**

_____

Place Value

hundred-millions | ten-millions | millions | hundred-thousands | ten-thousands | thousands | hundreds | tens | ones

$$9\ 5,\ 3\ 6\ 5,\ 0\ 0\ 0$$

Mexico has more than **95,365,000** people.
(ninety-five million, three hundred sixty-five thousand)

Write each number in standard form.

1. nine million, one hundred three thousand, two hundred five

   _____

2. four hundred thirty-three million, six hundred forty-seven thousand, one hundred twelve

   _____

3. seventeen million, two hundred twenty-one thousand, fifty

   _____

Tell what the place value of the **7** is in each number.

4. **3**7**9,882,154**   7 ten-millions

5. **17,205,148**   _____

6. **2,057,268**   _____

7. **508,672,304**   _____

8. **540,916,278**   _____

9. **7**89,544,912   _____

Rounding: Tens and Hundreds

When rounding to the nearest **10**, look at the ones place. **34** is between **30** and **40**, but it is closer to **30** so it is rounded down to **30**. **687** is between **680** and **690**, but it is closer to **690** so it is rounded up to **690**.

When rounding to the nearest **100**, look at the tens place. **583** is between **500** and **600**, but it is closer to **600** so it is rounded up to **600**. **5,221** is between **5,200** and **5,300**, but it is closer to **5,200** so it is rounded down to **5,200**.

When the number you are looking at is **0, 1, 2, 3,** or **4**, always round down. When the number you are looking at is **5, 6, 7, 8,** or **9**, always round up.

40
39
38
37
36
35
34
33
32
31
30

Collared lizard

Round each number to the nearest ten.

1. **43** _____   **685** _____   **942** _____

2. **86** _____   **251** _____   **804** _____

Round each number to the nearest hundred.

3. **378** _____   **542** _____   **439** _____

4. **1,894** _____   **2,358** _____   **750** _____

Fer-de-lance

Challenge: The area of all the land in Mexico is **756,066** square miles. What is the area rounded off to the nearest ten?

_____

What is the area rounded off to the nearest hundred?

_____

Rounding to the Nearest Thousand

When rounding to the nearest **1,000**, look at the hundreds place. If the number is **4** or below, round down. If the number is **5** or above, round up.

Mexico's population is about **95,365,100** people. **1** is in the hundreds place. Because **1** is less than **5**, the number **95,365,100** needs to be rounded down to **95,365,000**.

If you are rounding down, you do not change the number in the thousands place. If you are rounding up, you increase the number in the thousands place. The numbers behind the thousands place all become **0**.

Below is a list of some of the largest cities in Mexico and their populations. Round each population to the nearest thousand.

1. Mexico City   **15,525,000**   _____

2. Guadalajara   **1,650,205**   _____

3. Monterrey   **1,069,238**   _____

4. Puebla   **646,599**   _____

5. Juárez   **597,096**   _____

6. León   **589,950**   _____

7. Culiacán   **282,000**   _____

Round each number to the nearest thousand.

8. **3,468** _____   **6,843** _____   **7,621** _____

9. **5,033** _____   **942** _____   **72** _____

Using What You Know: Review

Compare the numbers. Use <, >, or =.

1. **362** ___ **356**   **6,137** ___ **2,814**

2. **9** x **6** ___ **86**   **6** x **6** ___ **9** x **4**

Write the numbers from least to greatest.

3. **3,859**   **3,921**   **3,666**   **2,901**   **505**   **3,877**

_____

Write each number in standard form.

Iguana

4. one million, two hundred eleven thousand, five hundred one

_____

5. sixty-two thousand, eighty-nine

_____

Tell what the **2** means in each number.

6. **827** _____   324,501 _____

Round to the nearest ten.

7. **46** _____   **132** _____   **91** _____   **98** _____

Round to the nearest hundred.

8. **620** _____   **1,890** _____   **87** _____   **7,888** _____

Round to the nearest thousand.

9. **54,890** _____   **809,114** _____   **905** _____

Estimating Sums

Try some **mental math**! Use your rounding off skills to **estimate**.

$476 + 121$ Think: **476** rounds up to **500**.
            121 rounds down to **100**.

500 + 100 is **600**.

So, **476 + 121** is about **600**.

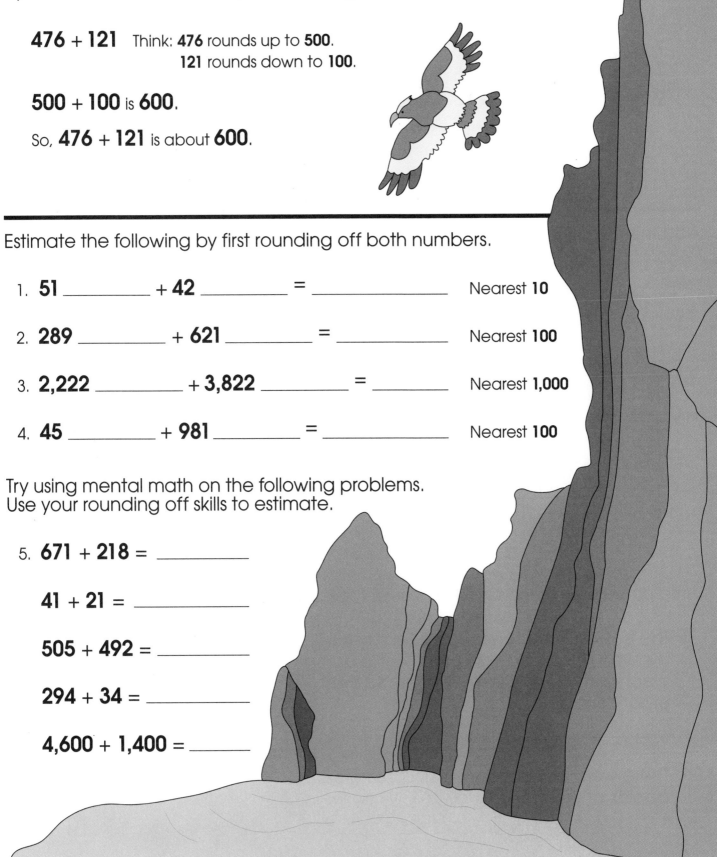

Estimate the following by first rounding off both numbers.

1. **51** _____ + **42** _____ = _____   Nearest **10**

2. **289** _____ + **621** _____ = _____   Nearest **100**

3. **2,222** _____ + **3,822** _____ = _____   Nearest **1,000**

4. **45** _____ + **981** _____ = _____   Nearest **100**

Try using mental math on the following problems.
Use your rounding off skills to estimate.

5. **671 + 218** = _____

   41 + 21 = _____

   505 + 492 = _____

   294 + 34 = _____

   4,600 + 1,400 = _____

Addition: Regrouping Once

$$
\begin{array}{r}
\overset{\text{tens}}{}\overset{\text{ones}}{} \\
1 \\
7\,8\cent \\
+1\,5\cent \\
\hline
9\,3\cent
\end{array}
$$

7 dimes + **8** pennies
+ **1** dime + **5** pennies
_____
8 dimes + **13** pennies =
8 dimes + **1** dime + **3** pennies =
9 dimes + **3** pennies

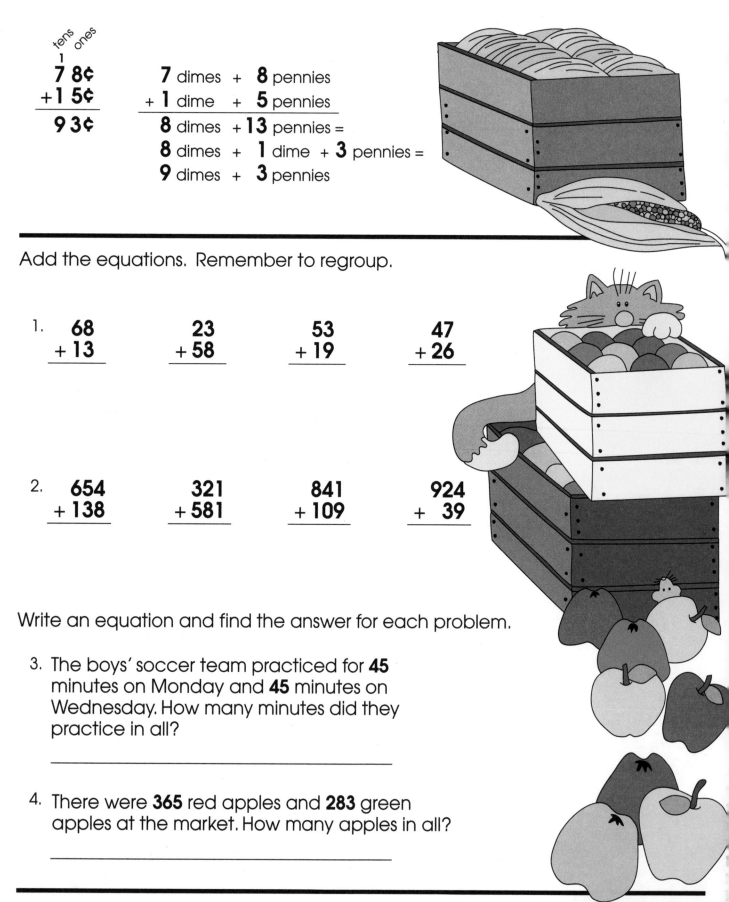

Add the equations. Remember to regroup.

1.
$$
\begin{array}{r} 68 \\ +13 \\ \hline \end{array}
\qquad
\begin{array}{r} 23 \\ +58 \\ \hline \end{array}
\qquad
\begin{array}{r} 53 \\ +19 \\ \hline \end{array}
\qquad
\begin{array}{r} 47 \\ +26 \\ \hline \end{array}
$$

2.
$$
\begin{array}{r} 654 \\ +138 \\ \hline \end{array}
\qquad
\begin{array}{r} 321 \\ +581 \\ \hline \end{array}
\qquad
\begin{array}{r} 841 \\ +109 \\ \hline \end{array}
\qquad
\begin{array}{r} 924 \\ +39 \\ \hline \end{array}
$$

Write an equation and find the answer for each problem.

3. The boys' soccer team practiced for **45** minutes on Monday and **45** minutes on Wednesday. How many minutes did they practice in all?

_____

4. There were **365** red apples and **283** green apples at the market. How many apples in all?

_____

Addition: Regrouping More Than Once

Add the ones.	Add the tens.	Add the hundreds.	Add the thousands.

$$\begin{array}{r} {\scriptstyle 1} \\ 3{,}7\,5\,4 \\ +\,1{,}8\,3\,7 \\ \hline 1 \end{array}$$
$$\begin{array}{r} {\scriptstyle 1} \\ 3{,}7\,5\,4 \\ +\,1{,}8\,3\,7 \\ \hline 9\,1 \end{array}$$
$$\begin{array}{r} {\scriptstyle 1}\;{\scriptstyle 1} \\ 3{,}7\,5\,4 \\ +\,1{,}8\,3\,7 \\ \hline 5\,9\,1 \end{array}$$
$$\begin{array}{r} {\scriptstyle 1}\;{\scriptstyle 1} \\ 3{,}7\,5\,4 \\ +\,1{,}8\,3\,7 \\ \hline 5{,}5\,9\,1 \end{array}$$

Solve each problem. Remember to regroup more than once.

1.
$$\begin{array}{r} 368 \\ +\,593 \\ \hline \end{array}$$
$$\begin{array}{r} 593 \\ +\,668 \\ \hline \end{array}$$
$$\begin{array}{r} 297 \\ +\,493 \\ \hline \end{array}$$
$$\begin{array}{r} 386 \\ +\,857 \\ \hline \end{array}$$

2.
$$\begin{array}{r} 3{,}333 \\ +\quad 777 \\ \hline \end{array}$$
$$\begin{array}{r} 9{,}054 \\ +\quad 857 \\ \hline \end{array}$$
$$\begin{array}{r} 3{,}289 \\ +\,1{,}931 \\ \hline \end{array}$$
$$\begin{array}{r} 8{,}721 \\ +\,1{,}189 \\ \hline \end{array}$$

Solve the problems.

3. Miguel is a mousetrap maker. Once he made **563** mousetraps out of bubblegum. He made another **447** mousetraps out of doorknobs. Quite the clever fellow! How many mousetraps did he make in all?

_____

4. Luis spends all day thinking. One day he thought of **1,599** funny jokes to tell his friends. His friend Pedro thought of **2,735** very funny jokes to tell. Was there ever a lot of laughing that day! How many jokes did their friends hear?

_____

Three or More Addends

When adding more than two numbers, look for sums of **10** to help you. Sometimes you can find a sum of **10** with numbers that are not next to each other.

$$
\begin{array}{r}
\overset{1}{3}\,7 \\
5\,6 \\
+\,5\,3 \\
\hline
1\,4\,6
\end{array}
$$

Add the ones.
$7 + 3 = 10.$ $10 + 6 = 16.$
Regroup.
Add the tens.
$5 + 5 = 10.$ $10 + 3 + 1 = 14.$

Add the equations.

1.
$$
\begin{array}{r}
12 \\
6 \\
+\,94
\end{array}
\qquad
\begin{array}{r}
70 \\
19 \\
+\,31
\end{array}
\qquad
\begin{array}{r}
4 \\
59 \\
+\,46
\end{array}
\qquad
\begin{array}{r}
32 \\
16 \\
+\,78
\end{array}
$$

2.
$$
\begin{array}{r}
105 \\
347 \\
+\,555
\end{array}
\qquad
\begin{array}{r}
392 \\
747 \\
+\,741
\end{array}
\qquad
\begin{array}{r}
3{,}162 \\
6{,}392 \\
+\,4{,}818
\end{array}
\qquad
\begin{array}{r}
1{,}322 \\
7{,}411 \\
+\,1{,}078
\end{array}
$$

Solve the story problem.

3. Melinda loved to read. First she read a book about Mexico with **250** pages. Then she read a joke book with **97** pages. Last she read a poetry book with **453** pages. How many pages did she read in all?

_____

Subtraction with Renaming

$$\begin{array}{r} 5\,4 \\ -\,2\,6 \\ \hline \end{array}$$

Always start with the top number.
You cannot take **6** away from **4**.
You must rename from the tens.

$$\begin{array}{r} {}^{4}\!\!\not5\,4 \\ -\,2\,6 \\ \hline \end{array}$$

Rename **1** ten from the **5** tens.
5 – 1 = 4 tens.
There are now **4** tens.

$$\begin{array}{r} {}^{4}\!\!\not5\,{}^{14}\!\!4 \\ -\,2\,6 \\ \hline \end{array}$$

Add the **1** ten to the **4** ones.
10 + 4 = 14 ones.
There are now **14** ones.

$$\begin{array}{r} {}^{4}\!\!\not5\,{}^{14}\!\!4 \\ -\,2\,6 \\ \hline 2\,8 \end{array}$$

Now you're ready to subtract.
14 take away **6**.
4 take away **2**.

$$\begin{array}{r} 2\,8 \\ +\,2\,6 \\ \hline 5\,4 \end{array}$$

To check your answer, add the difference (answer) to the number you subtracted.

Popocatepetl
volcano

Subtract using renaming.
Check your answers.

		Check		Check		Check
1.	$\begin{array}{r}65\\-48\\\hline\end{array}$	+ ____	$\begin{array}{r}92\\-56\\\hline\end{array}$	+ ____	$\begin{array}{r}43\\-37\\\hline\end{array}$	+ ____

		Check		Check		Check
2.	$\begin{array}{r}84\\-39\\\hline\end{array}$	+ ____	$\begin{array}{r}78\\-59\\\hline\end{array}$	+ ____	$\begin{array}{r}55\\-17\\\hline\end{array}$	+ ____

Renaming for Subtraction

Rename **4,392** to show **10** more ones.

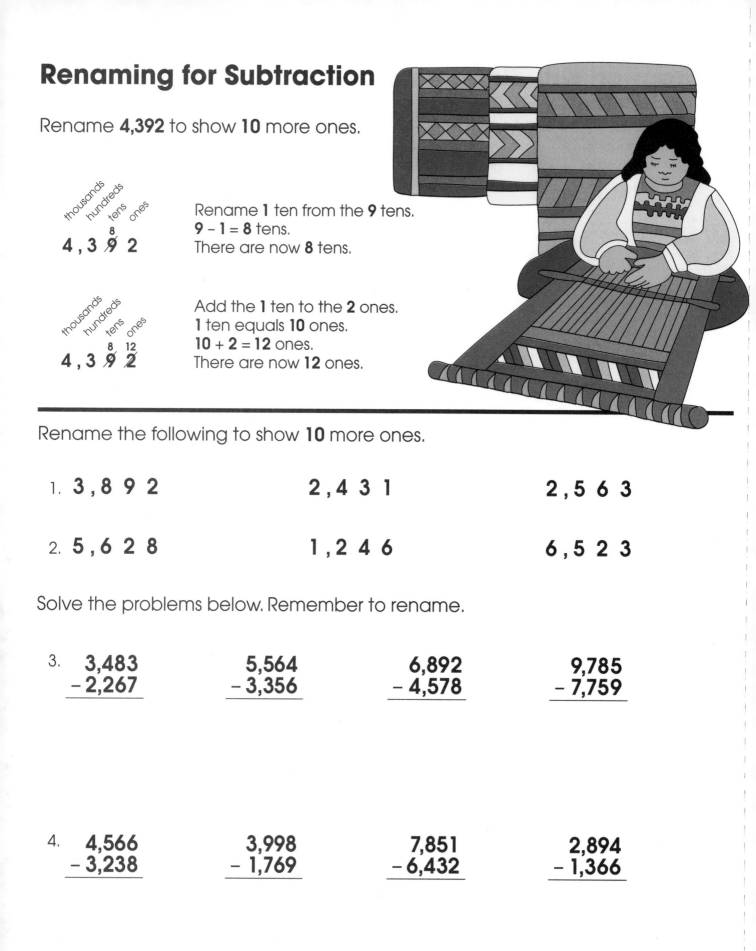

thousands hundreds tens ones

8
4 , 3 9̸ 2

Rename **1** ten from the **9** tens.
9 – 1 = 8 tens.
There are now **8** tens.

thousands hundreds tens ones

8 12
4 , 3 9̸ 2̸

Add the **1** ten to the **2** ones.
1 ten equals **10** ones.
10 + 2 = 12 ones.
There are now **12** ones.

Rename the following to show **10** more ones.

1. **3 , 8 9 2**   **2 , 4 3 1**   **2 , 5 6 3**

2. **5 , 6 2 8**   **1 , 2 4 6**   **6 , 5 2 3**

Solve the problems below. Remember to rename.

3. 3,483   5,564   6,892   9,785
  – 2,267   – 3,356   – 4,578   – 7,759

4. 4,566   3,998   7,851   2,894
  – 3,238   – 1,769   – 6,432   – 1,366

Renaming for Subtraction

Rename **9,861** to show **10** more tens.

thousands hundreds tens ones

    7

9,8 6 1

Rename **1** hundred from the **8** hundreds.
8 – 1 = 7 hundreds.
There are now **7** hundreds.

thousands hundreds tens ones

    7 16

9,8 6 1

Add the **1** hundred to the **6** tens.
1 hundred equals **10** tens.
10 + 6 = 16 tens.
There are now **16** tens.

Rename the following to show **10** more tens.

1. **2 , 2 2 2**   **6 , 4 2 7**   **1 , 3 7 3**

2. **6 , 1 5 1**   **3 , 2 1 3**   **5 , 7 2 6**

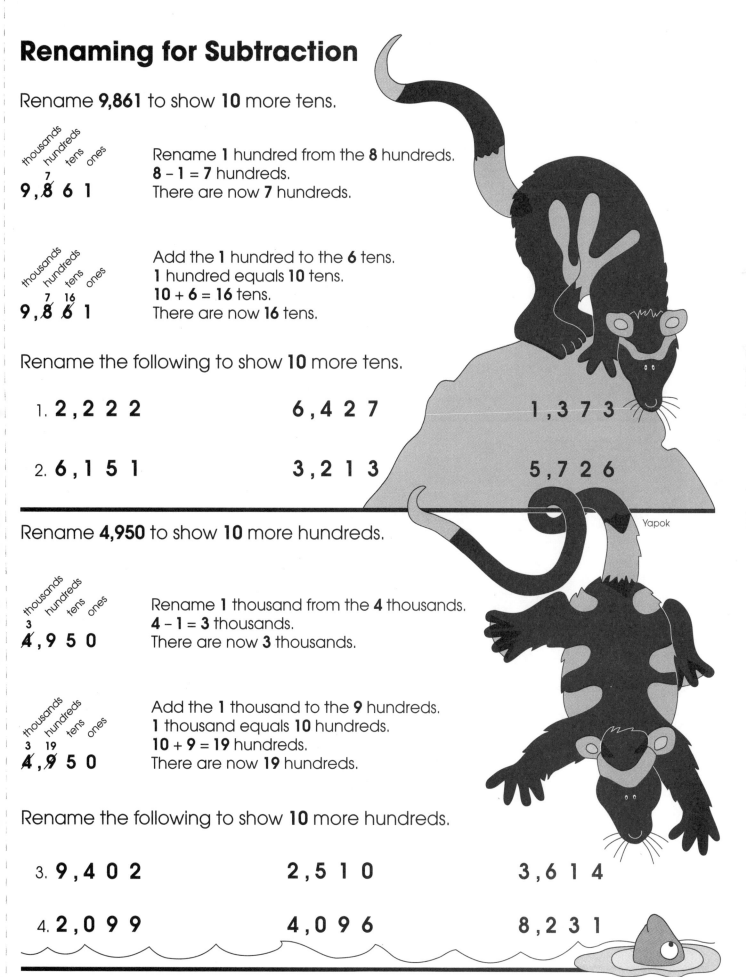

Yapok

Rename **4,950** to show **10** more hundreds.

thousands hundreds tens ones

3

4,9 5 0

Rename **1** thousand from the **4** thousands.
4 – 1 = 3 thousands.
There are now **3** thousands.

thousands hundreds tens ones

3 19

4,9 5 0

Add the **1** thousand to the **9** hundreds.
1 thousand equals **10** hundreds.
10 + 9 = 19 hundreds.
There are now **19** hundreds.

Rename the following to show **10** more hundreds.

3. **9 , 4 0 2**   **2 , 5 1 0**   **3 , 6 1 4**

4. **2 , 0 9 9**   **4 , 0 9 6**   **8 , 2 3 1**

Subtraction: Renaming More Than Once

$$
\begin{array}{r}
\overset{2}{\cancel{2}}\overset{14}{\cancel{3}}4 \\
-\ 1\ 4\ 8 \\
\hline
6
\end{array}
$$

8 ones cannot be subtracted from **4** ones. Rename to show **10** more ones.

$$
\begin{array}{r}
\overset{1}{\cancel{2}}\overset{12}{\cancel{3}}\overset{14}{\cancel{4}} \\
-\ 1\ 4\ 8 \\
\hline
8\ 6
\end{array}
$$

4 tens cannot be subtracted from **2** tens. Rename to show **10** more tens.

$$
\begin{array}{r}
\overset{1}{\cancel{2}}\overset{12}{\cancel{3}}\overset{14}{\cancel{4}} \\
-\ 1\ 4\ 8 \\
\hline
8\ 6
\end{array}
$$

Subtract the hundreds.

Subtract using renaming.

1.
$$
\begin{array}{r} 736 \\ -\ 349 \\ \hline \end{array}
\qquad
\begin{array}{r} 8,127 \\ -\ 675 \\ \hline \end{array}
\qquad
\begin{array}{r} 7,194 \\ -\ 1,856 \\ \hline \end{array}
\qquad
\begin{array}{r} 340 \\ -\ 93 \\ \hline \end{array}
$$

2.
$$
\begin{array}{r} 6,354 \\ -\ 5,888 \\ \hline \end{array}
\qquad
\begin{array}{r} 3,447 \\ -\ 1,299 \\ \hline \end{array}
\qquad
\begin{array}{r} 4,253 \\ -\ 2,444 \\ \hline \end{array}
\qquad
\begin{array}{r} 9,876 \\ -\ 3,877 \\ \hline \end{array}
$$

3.
$$
\begin{array}{r} 1,623 \\ -\ 766 \\ \hline \end{array}
\qquad
\begin{array}{r} 7,561 \\ -\ 2,654 \\ \hline \end{array}
\qquad
\begin{array}{r} 6,276 \\ -\ 559 \\ \hline \end{array}
\qquad
\begin{array}{r} 1,784 \\ -\ 795 \\ \hline \end{array}
$$

Subtraction: Renaming with Zeros

When there are no ones or tens, first rename to show **10** tens.

$$\begin{array}{r} 5,\overset{4}{\cancel{5}}\overset{10}{0}0 \\ -2,376 \\ \hline \end{array}$$

Next, rename to show **10** ones. Then subtract.

$$\begin{array}{r} 5,\overset{4}{\cancel{5}}\overset{9}{\cancel{0}}\overset{10}{0} \\ -2,376 \\ \hline 3,124 \end{array}$$

Try it!

1.
$$\begin{array}{r} 204 \\ -117 \\ \hline \end{array}$$
$$\begin{array}{r} 408 \\ -29 \\ \hline \end{array}$$
$$\begin{array}{r} 800 \\ -529 \\ \hline \end{array}$$
$$\begin{array}{r} 503 \\ -56 \\ \hline \end{array}$$

2.
$$\begin{array}{r} 6,700 \\ -5,379 \\ \hline \end{array}$$
$$\begin{array}{r} 7,020 \\ -443 \\ \hline \end{array}$$
$$\begin{array}{r} 5,002 \\ -661 \\ \hline \end{array}$$
$$\begin{array}{r} 6,000 \\ -1,278 \\ \hline \end{array}$$

Solve the problem.

3. In **1521**, Hernando Cortés conquered Mexico for Spain. Then in **1810**, Miguel Hidalgo y Costilla fought for Mexico's freedom from Spain. How many years did Spain rule Mexico before the fight for Mexico's freedom began? _____

Addition and Subtraction Review

To discover one of the best known Indian civilizations in Mexico, solve each problem. Then fill in the blanks at the bottom of the page with the correct letters.

1. Estimate each number to the nearest ten. **442 + 316**
   Write the new equation and answer. _____
   If your answer is over **750**, put an *A* in the blank.
   If your answer is under **750**, put a *P* in the blank.

2. **648**
   + 237
   If your answer is over **880**, put a *Z* in the blank.
   If your answer is under **880**, put a *G* in the blank.

3. **5,639**
   + 1,374
   If your answer is over **7,100**, put an *S* in the blank.
   If your answer is under **7,100**, put a *T* in the blank.

4. **392**
   400
   68
   + 715
   If your answer is over **1,500**, put an *E* in the blank.
   If your answer is under **1,500**, put an *O* in the blank.

5. Rename to show **10** more ones: **37** _____

   If your answer is **3** tens + **17** ones, put a *B* in the blank.
   If your answer is **2** tens + **17** ones, put a *C* in the blank.

6. **4,205**
   − 1,876
   If your answer is over **2,500**, put a *D* in the blank.
   If your answer is under **2,500**, put an *S* in the blank.

___   ___   ___   ___   ___   ___
1   2   3   4   5   6

Multiplication with Zeros

When multiplying with zeros, use mental math.

5 x 30

Think of the problem without the zero: **5 x 3.**
Your mental math tells you the product is **15.**
Now, add the zero onto the end for the answer: **150.**

5 x 30 = 150

It's just as easy with more zeros!

40 x 90

Think of the problem without the zeros: **4 x 9.**
Your mental math tells you the product is **36.**
Now, add both of the zeros onto the end for the answer: **3,600.**

40 x 90 = 3,600

When multiplying **3** numbers together, see if you can find two of them that make a multiple of ten for an answer. Then multiply by the third number.

9 x 8 x 5 =

Think **8 x 5 = 40**, then **9 x 40 = 360.**

Find the products.

1. **10 x 6 = _____**   **20 x 80 = _____**   **300 x 6 = _____**

2. **49 x 100 = _____**   **500 x 60 = _____**   **6 x 2,000 = _____**

3. **70 x 70 = _____**   **80 x 5 = _____**   **900 x 20 = _____**

4. **10 x 10 = _____**   **2 x 5 x 8 = _____**   **6 x 6 x 5 = _____**

5. **9 x 8 x 5 = _____**   **2 x 10 x 10 = _____**   **4 x 7 x 5 = _____**

Multiplication: No Regrouping

Multiply the ones.

$$\begin{array}{r} 4,321 \\ \times\ \ \ \ \ 3 \\ \hline 3 \end{array}$$

Multiply the tens.

$$\begin{array}{r} 4,321 \\ \times\ \ \ \ \ 3 \\ \hline 63 \end{array}$$

Multiply the hundreds.

$$\begin{array}{r} 4,321 \\ \times\ \ \ \ \ 3 \\ \hline 963 \end{array}$$

Multiply the thousands.

$$\begin{array}{r} 4,321 \\ \times\ \ \ \ \ 3 \\ \hline 12,963 \end{array}$$

Find the products.

1.
$$\begin{array}{r} 24 \\ \times\ 2 \\ \hline \end{array}$$
$$\begin{array}{r} 91 \\ \times\ 8 \\ \hline \end{array}$$
$$\begin{array}{r} 62 \\ \times\ 4 \\ \hline \end{array}$$

2.
$$\begin{array}{r} 501 \\ \times\ 7 \\ \hline \end{array}$$
$$\begin{array}{r} 813 \\ \times\ 3 \\ \hline \end{array}$$
$$\begin{array}{r} 732 \\ \times\ 3 \\ \hline \end{array}$$

3.
$$\begin{array}{r} 7,310 \\ \times\ 2 \\ \hline \end{array}$$
$$\begin{array}{r} 9,141 \\ \times\ 2 \\ \hline \end{array}$$
$$\begin{array}{r} 6,222 \\ \times\ 4 \\ \hline \end{array}$$

Solve the problems.

4. The average number of people living in one house in Mexico is **6**. In a small village, there are about **410** houses. How many people are living in the small village?

_____

5. Enrico had **4** hoses. Each was **42** feet long. How long were they when he hooked them all together?

_____

Multiplication: No Regrouping

Multiplication: Regrouping Once

Multiply the ones. Regroup the **15** ones as **1** ten and **5** ones.

$$\begin{array}{r} {\scriptstyle 1} \\ 2\,5 \\ \times\ \ 3 \\ \hline 5 \end{array}$$

Multiply the tens. Add the extra ten to the total.

$$\begin{array}{r} {\scriptstyle 1} \\ 2\,5 \\ \times\ \ 3 \\ \hline 7\,5 \end{array}$$

Gray whale

Multiply to find the products.

1.
$$\begin{array}{r} 58 \\ \times\ 4 \\ \hline \end{array}$$
$$\begin{array}{r} 17 \\ \times\ 6 \\ \hline \end{array}$$
$$\begin{array}{r} 73 \\ \times\ 8 \\ \hline \end{array}$$

2.
$$\begin{array}{r} 272 \\ \times\ \ \ 3 \\ \hline \end{array}$$
$$\begin{array}{r} 970 \\ \times\ \ \ 7 \\ \hline \end{array}$$
$$\begin{array}{r} 381 \\ \times\ \ \ 2 \\ \hline \end{array}$$

3.
$$\begin{array}{r} 1,522 \\ \times\ \ \ \ \ 3 \\ \hline \end{array}$$
$$\begin{array}{r} 9,071 \\ \times\ \ \ \ \ 6 \\ \hline \end{array}$$
$$\begin{array}{r} 4,003 \\ \times\ \ \ \ \ 9 \\ \hline \end{array}$$

Solve the problem.

4. There are **24** hours in a day. There are **7** days in one week. How many hours are there in one week? _____

Multiplication: Regrouping More Than Once

Multiply the ones.

```
    1
  3 6 4
x     4
─────────
      6
```

4 x 4 = 16 ones.
16 = 1 ten and **6** ones.

Multiply the tens.

```
  2 1
  3 6 4
x     4
─────────
    5 6
```

4 x 6 = 24 tens.
24 tens + **1** ten = **25** tens.
25 tens = **2** hundreds and **5** tens.

Multiply the hundreds.

```
  2 1
  3 6 4
x     4
─────────
1, 4 5 6
```

4 x 3 = 12 hundreds.
12 hundreds + **2** hundreds = **14** hundreds.

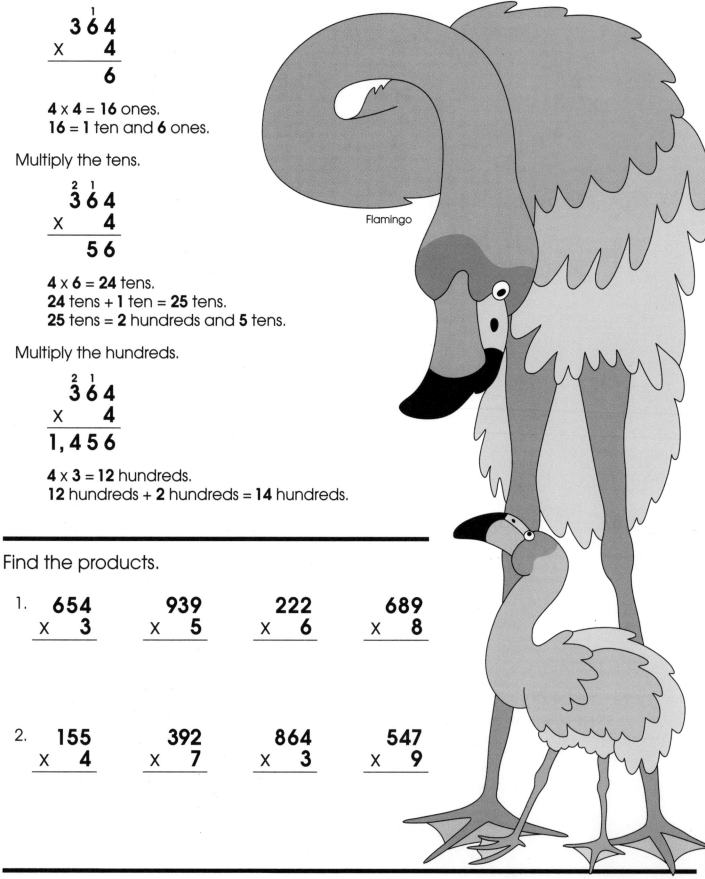

Flamingo

───────────────────────────

Find the products.

1.
```
  654        939        222        689
x   3      x   5      x   6      x   8
```

2.
```
  155        392        864        547
x   4      x   7      x   3      x   9
```

Multiplication: Regrouping with Zeros

Multiply the ones.

$$
\begin{array}{r}
5\overset{2}{0}4 \\
\times\quad 6 \\
\hline
4
\end{array}
$$

24 = 2 tens and 4 ones.

Multiply the tens.

$$
\begin{array}{r}
5\overset{2}{0}4 \\
\times\quad 6 \\
\hline
24
\end{array}
$$

0 tens + 2 tens = 2 tens.

Multiply the hundreds.

$$
\begin{array}{r}
5\overset{2}{0}4 \\
\times\quad 6 \\
\hline
3,024
\end{array}
$$

5 x 6 = 30 hundreds.

Find the products.

1.
$$
\begin{array}{r} 560 \\ \times\ 5 \\ \hline \end{array}
\qquad
\begin{array}{r} 601 \\ \times\ 8 \\ \hline \end{array}
\qquad
\begin{array}{r} 302 \\ \times\ 5 \\ \hline \end{array}
\qquad
\begin{array}{r} 809 \\ \times\ 3 \\ \hline \end{array}
$$

2.
$$
\begin{array}{r} 2,002 \\ \times\ 7 \\ \hline \end{array}
\qquad
\begin{array}{r} 7,050 \\ \times\ 4 \\ \hline \end{array}
\qquad
\begin{array}{r} 8,007 \\ \times\ 2 \\ \hline \end{array}
\qquad
\begin{array}{r} 5,060 \\ \times\ 9 \\ \hline \end{array}
$$

Solve the problems.

3. Many Mexican craft workers make beautiful pottery and glassware, which they sell to tourists. If some tourists bought **8** pieces of pottery, and each piece sold for **$205**, what would the total price be?

   _____

4. The distance from Mexico City to Córdoba is about **170** miles. If someone made this trip **5** times, how many miles would the person travel?

   _____

Multiplication with Two-Digit Multipliers

Think of **23** as **20 + 3**.

$$\begin{array}{r} 5\,4 \\ \times\ 2\,3 \\ \end{array}$$

Multiply **54 x 3**.

$$\begin{array}{r} {}^{1} \\ 5\,4 \\ \times\ 2\,3 \\ \hline 1\,6\,2 \\ \end{array}$$

Multiply **54 x 20**.
Remember mental math with
the zero. **2 x 4 = 8   2 x 5 = 10**.
Add together.

$$\begin{array}{r} 5\,4 \\ \times\ 2\,3 \\ \hline 1\,6\,2 \\ 1\,0\,8\,0 \\ \hline 1,2\,4\,2 \\ \end{array}$$

Put the zero in
the ones place.

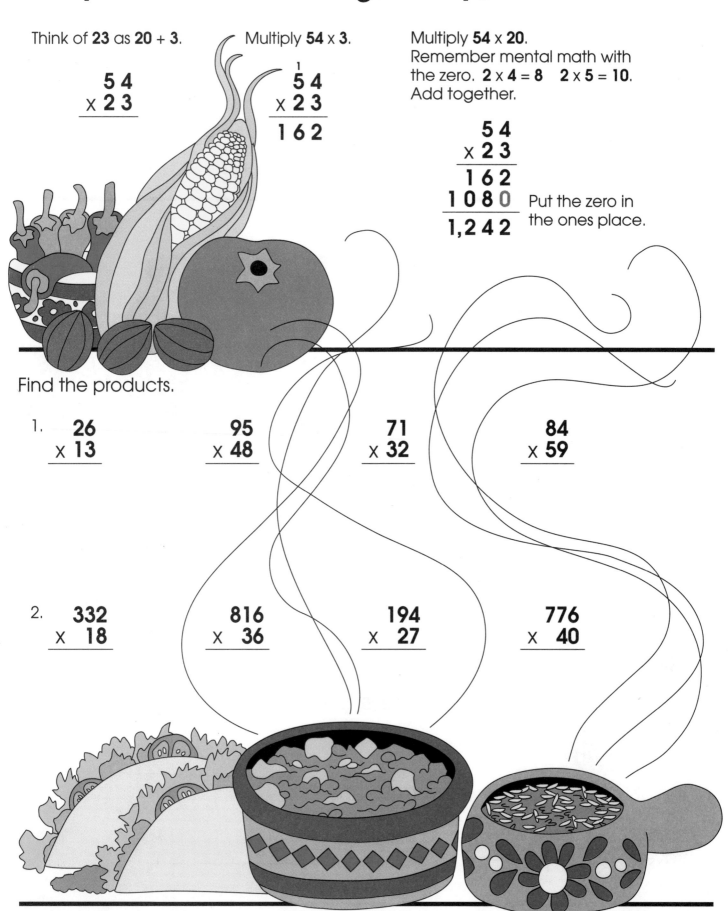

Find the products.

1.
$$\begin{array}{r} 26 \\ \times\ 13 \\ \end{array}$$
$$\begin{array}{r} 95 \\ \times\ 48 \\ \end{array}$$
$$\begin{array}{r} 71 \\ \times\ 32 \\ \end{array}$$
$$\begin{array}{r} 84 \\ \times\ 59 \\ \end{array}$$

2.
$$\begin{array}{r} 332 \\ \times\ 18 \\ \end{array}$$
$$\begin{array}{r} 816 \\ \times\ 36 \\ \end{array}$$
$$\begin{array}{r} 194 \\ \times\ 27 \\ \end{array}$$
$$\begin{array}{r} 776 \\ \times\ 40 \\ \end{array}$$

Division Facts

Divide is the opposite of *multiply*.
Multiplication is combining groups together.
Division is separating the groups.
When you see a division fact problem
like **48 ÷ 6 =**, ask yourself **6 x ? = 48**.

Solve the division problems. Write the multiplication
problems that go with the division problems.

1. **18 ÷ 3 =** _____6_____   _____6 × 3 = 18_____

2. **36 ÷ 9 =** _____   _____

3. **54 ÷ 6 =** _____   _____

4. **9 ÷ 3 =** _____   _____

5. **28 ÷ 7 =** _____   _____

6. **40 ÷ 10 =** _____   _____

7. **121 ÷ 11 =** _____   _____

8. **84 ÷ 12 =** _____   _____

9. **15 ÷ 3 =** _____   _____

10. **144 ÷ 12 =** _____   _____

11. **60 ÷ 10 =** _____   _____

12. **44 ÷ 4 =** _____   _____

Giant ahuehuete

Division

Below are several Mexican objects. To solve the problems within each object, divide the numbers by the center number. The arrows show you where to write your answers.

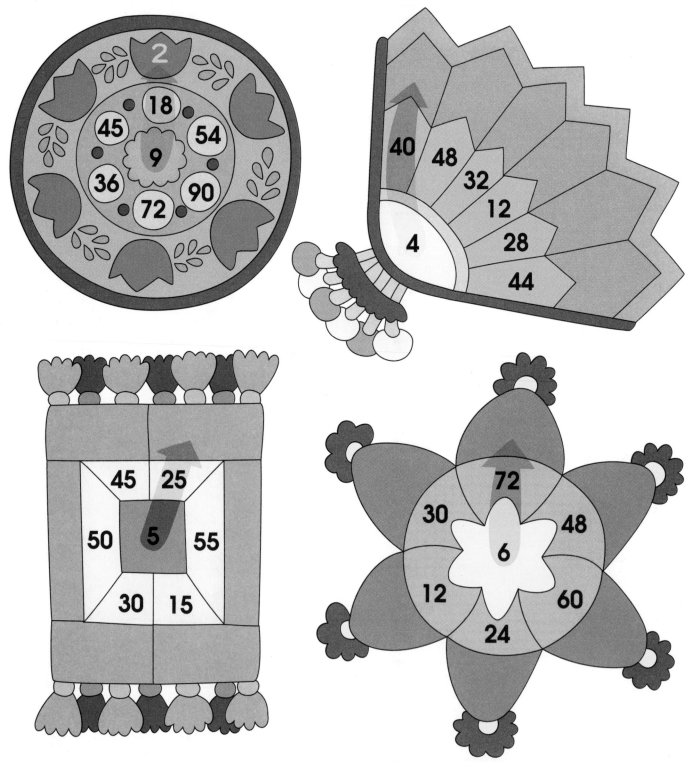

Practice your division facts so you can say them fast!

Remainders

3 words to know:
dividend – the number being divided
divisor – the number of times the dividend is being separated
quotient – the answer

$$12 \div 3 = 4$$

dividend ÷ divisor = quotient

Another word to know:
remainder – what is left over after the dividend
is divided by the divisor

```
   4 R2
 3| 14
  -12
    2
```

```
    4
  x 3
   12
  + 2
   14
```

Divide **14 ÷ 3**. Write **4** above the **4**.
Multiply. **4 x 3 = 12**.
Subtract. **14 – 12 = 2**.
The remainder is **2**. Write R**2** next to the answer.
The remainder must be less than the divisor.

$$14 \div 3 = 4 \ \textbf{R2}$$

Check:
To check, multiply the quotient (answer)
by the divisor, then add the remainder.
This will equal the dividend.

Find the quotients. (Every answer below will have a remainder.)
Then check your answers.

1.
Check
$5\overline{)19}$ x _____

+ _____

Check
$9\overline{)46}$ x _____

+ _____

Check
$6\overline{)8}$ x _____

+ _____

2.
Check
$3\overline{)22}$ x _____

+ _____

Check
$8\overline{)71}$ x _____

+ _____

Check
$7\overline{)39}$ x _____

+ _____

Two-Digit Quotients

$$
\begin{array}{r}
1 \\
5\overline{)73} \\
-5 \\
\hline
2
\end{array}
$$

Divide. $7 \div 5 = 1$
Write **1** above the tens.
Multiply. $1 \times 5 = 5$
Subtract. $7 - 5 = 2$

$$
\begin{array}{r}
14\,\text{R}3 \\
5\overline{)73} \\
-5 \\
\hline
23 \\
-20 \\
\hline
3
\end{array}
$$

Bring down the next digit in the dividend (**3**).
Divide. $23 \div 5 = 4$
Write **4** above the ones.
Multiply. $4 \times 5 = 20$
Subtract. $23 - 20 = 3$
Make sure your remainder
is smaller than the divisor (**5**).
Write the remainder next to the answer.

Parnell's mustached bat

$$
\begin{array}{r}
14 \\
\times\ 5 \\
\hline
70 \\
+\ 3 \\
\hline
73
\end{array}
$$

Check.
To check, multiply the quotient (answer)
by the divisor. Then add the remainder.
This will equal the dividend.

Vampire bat

Find the quotients.

1.

| $4\overline{)91}$ | Check $\times$ ___
 $+$ ___ | $6\overline{)89}$ | Check $\times$ ___
 $+$ ___ | $3\overline{)77}$ | Check $\times$ ___
 $+$ ___ |

2.

| $7\overline{)88}$ | Check $\times$ ___
 $+$ ___ | $2\overline{)63}$ | Check $\times$ ___
 $+$ ___ | $5\overline{)96}$ | Check $\times$ ___
 $+$ ___ |

Decimals

This shaded area can be written as $1\frac{6}{10}$.

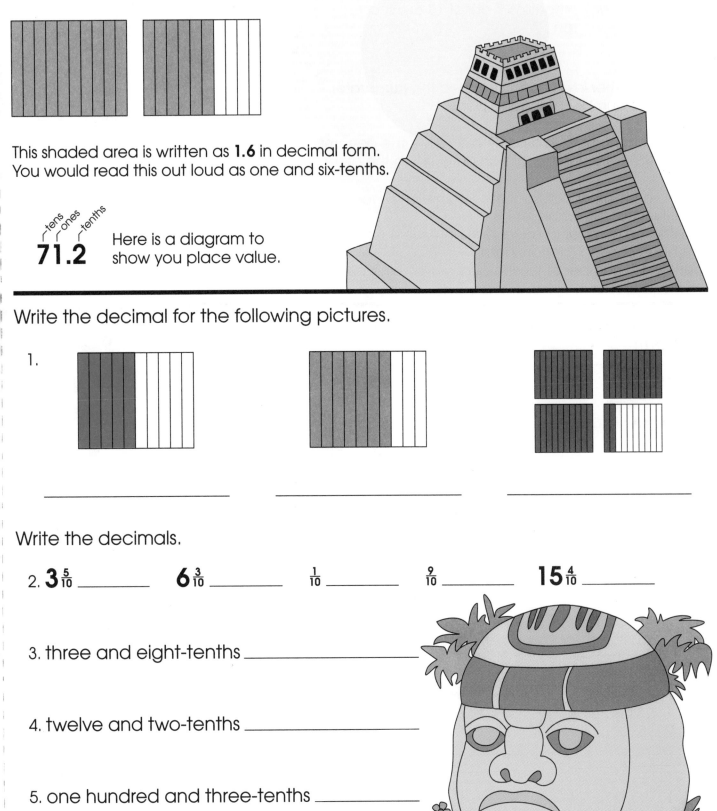

This shaded area is written as **1.6** in decimal form.
You would read this out loud as one and six-tenths.

tens ones tenths
71.2   Here is a diagram to show you place value.

Write the decimal for the following pictures.

1.

_____   _____   _____

Write the decimals.

2. $3\frac{5}{10}$ _____ $6\frac{3}{10}$ _____ $\frac{1}{10}$ _____ $\frac{9}{10}$ _____ $15\frac{4}{10}$ _____

3. three and eight-tenths _____

4. twelve and two-tenths _____

5. one hundred and three-tenths _____

Fractions

Fractions are another way of showing part of a whole.
Look at the stack of tortillas. **7** out of **10** are shaded.
The fraction is written $\dfrac{7}{10}$.

If I can talk, you can do this!

The top number in a fraction is called the **numerator**.
It gives the number of shaded parts.

The bottom number in a fraction is called the **denominator**.
It gives the total number of parts into which the object is divided.

When you think about fractions, you need to do three things:
Identify what the whole or **1** is.
Identify the number of equal parts into which the whole
has been divided (denominator).
Identify the number of those equal parts being considered (numerator).

Write the fractions for the pictures below.

1. _____   _____

2. _____   _____

Scarlet macaw

What is the numerator in the following fractions?

3. $\dfrac{1}{5}$ _____ $\dfrac{7}{10}$ _____ $\dfrac{5}{6}$ _____

What is the denominator in the following fractions?

4. $\dfrac{4}{10}$ _____ $\dfrac{1}{4}$ _____ $\dfrac{6}{7}$ _____

Draw a picture of the following fractions.

5. $\dfrac{2}{3}$ $\dfrac{6}{6}$

6. $\dfrac{1}{5}$ $\dfrac{3}{4}$

Comparing Fractions

For fractions to be compared, the denominators must be the same. The fraction with the larger numerator shows the greater amount.
3/4 is larger than **2/4**.

How did this child spend the day?

Sleep	**8/24**
Meals	**2/24**
School	**6/24**
Work	**4/24**
Leisure	**4/24**

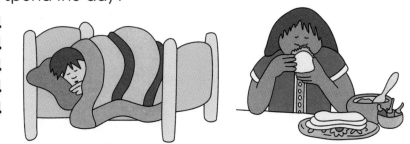

Answer the following questions by using the chart above.

1. What did this child do most in a **24**-hour day? _____

2. What took the least time? _____

3. Did this child spend more time in school or more time working?

_____

Compare the numbers using <, >, or = .

4. $\dfrac{3}{4}$ _____ $\dfrac{5}{4}$ 1 _____ $\dfrac{2}{3}$

5. $\dfrac{9}{10}$ _____ $\dfrac{6}{10}$ $\dfrac{6}{7}$ _____ $\dfrac{5}{7}$

6. $\dfrac{4}{8}$ _____ $\dfrac{7}{8}$ $\dfrac{1}{4}$ _____ 1

7. Draw **2** tortillas. Divide them each into **8** equal parts. Shade in **3/8** on one and **4/8** on the other. Circle the one that has more parts shaded in.

Adding Fractions

When adding fractions, add only the numerators.
The denominator remains the same.
The denominator serves as a label that tells you what kind of
fractions are being added. You do not need to add the labels.

$$\frac{1}{3} + \frac{1}{3} = \frac{2}{3}$$

Add the following fractions.

1. $\frac{2}{7} + \frac{4}{7} =$ _____

2. $\frac{1}{4} + \frac{3}{4} =$ _____

3. $\frac{1}{10} + \frac{7}{10} =$ _____

4. $\frac{3}{9} + \frac{4}{9} =$ _____

| 0/2 | | | 1/2 | | | 2/2 |

| 0/4 | 1/4 | 2/4 | 3/4 | 4/4 |

| 0/8 | 1/8 | 2/8 | 3/8 | 4/8 | 5/8 | 6/8 | 7/8 | 8/8 |

Look at the number line to find equal fractions. **1/4 = 2/8**

5. What are **2** other fractions that equal **1/2**? _____

6. What is another fraction that equals **6/8**? _____

7. **2/2 = 4/4 = 8/8**. What whole number do all these fractions equal? _____

Answer Key

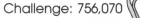

Page 33
1. > 2. > 3. >
   <   <   =
   <   <   <
4. 149; 287; 324; 822
5. 2,118; 2,973; 3,006; 3,652
6. 2,821; 2,840; 4,431; 4,931
7.   135   310   560
   Juanita Lucia Maria

Page 34
1.   3 5 0
2. 1 8 8 0
3. 5 5 0 0
4.   7,432
5.   6,341
6.   1,095

Page 35
1. 9,103,205
2. 433,647,112
3. 17,221,050
4. 7 ten-millions
5. 7 millions
6. 7 thousands
7. 7 ten-thousands
8. 7 tens
9. 7 hundred-millions

Page 36
1. 40; 690; 940
2. 90; 250; 800
3. 400; 500; 400
4. 1,900; 2,400; 800
Challenge: 756,070
          756,100

Page 37
1. 15,525,000
2. 1,650,000
3. 1,069,000
4. 647,000
5. 597,000
6. 590,000
7. 282,000
8. 3,000; 7,000; 8,000
9. 5,000; 1,000; 0

Page 38
1. >, >
2. <, =
3. 505; 2,901; 3,666; 3,859; 3,877; 3,921
4. 1,211,501
5. 62,089
6. 2 tens; 2 ten-thousands
7. 50; 130; 90; 100
8. 600; 1,900; 100; 7,900
9. 55,000; 809,000; 1,000

Page 39
1. 50 + 40 = 90
2. 300 + 600 = 900
3. 2,000 + 4,000 = 6,000
4. 0 + 1,000 = 1,000
5.   900
      60
  1,000
    330
  6,000

Page 40
1. 81, 81, 72, 73
2. 792, 902, 950, 963
3. 45 + 45 = 90 minutes
4. 365 + 283 = 648 apples

Page 41
1. 961; 1,261; 790; 1,243
2. 4,110; 9,911; 5,220; 9,910
3. 1,010 mousetraps
4. 4,334 jokes

Page 42
1. 112; 120; 109; 126
2. 1,007; 1,880; 14,372; 9,811
3. 800 pages

Page 43
1. 17, 36, 6
2. 45, 19, 38

Page 44
1. 3,8⁸9̶¹²2̶   2,4³3̶¹¹X̶   2,5⁵6̶¹³3̶
2. 5,6²2̶¹⁸8̶   1,2³4̶¹⁶6̶   6,5²2̶¹³3̶
3. 1,216   2,208   2,314   2,026
4. 1,328   2,229   1,419   1,528

Page 45
1. 2,¹2̶¹²2̶2   6,4²2̶¹²7̶   1,³3̶¹²7̶3̶
2. 6,⁰X̶¹⁵5̶1   3,²2̶¹¹1̶3   5,⁶7̶¹²2̶6̶
3. ⁸9̶¹⁴,4̶02   2,²5̶¹⁶1̶0   3,⁶6̶¹⁶1̶4
4. ¹2̶¹⁰,Ø99   ³4̶¹⁰,Ø96   8,⁷2̶¹²3̶1

Page 46
1. 387; 7,452; 5,338; 247
2. 466; 2,148; 1,809; 5,999
3. 857; 4,907; 5,717; 989

Page 47
1. 87; 379; 271; 447
2. 1,321; 6,577; 4,341; 4722
3. 289 years

Answer Key

Answer Key

Page 48
1. 440 + 320 = 760
2. 885
3. 7,013
4. 1,575
5. 2 tens + 17 ones
6. 2,329
   AZTECS

Page 49
1. 60; 1,600; 1,800
2. 4,900; 30,000; 12,000
3. 4,900; 400; 18,000
4. 100; 80; 180
5. 360; 200; 140

Page 50
1. 48; 728; 248
2. 3,507; 2,439; 2,196
3. 14,620; 18,282; 24,888
4. 2,460 people
5. 168 feet

Page 51
1. 232; 102; 584
2. 816; 6,790; 762
3. 4,566; 54,426; 36,027
4. 168 hours

Page 52
1. 1,962; 4,695; 1,332; 5,512
2. 620; 2,744; 2,592; 4,923

Page 53
1. 2,800; 4,808; 1,510; 2,427
2. 14,014; 28,200; 16,014; 45,540
3. $1,640
4. 850 miles

Page 54
1. 338; 4,560; 2,272; 4,956
2. 5,976; 29,376; 5,238; 31,040

Page 55
1. 6, 6 x 3 = 18
2. 4, 4 x 9 = 36
3. 9, 9 x 6 = 54
4. 3, 3 x 3 = 9
5. 4, 4 x 7 = 28
6. 4, 4 x 10 = 40
7. 11, 11 x 11 = 121
8. 7, 7 x 12 = 84
9. 5, 5 x 3 = 15
10. 12, 12 x 12 = 144
11. 6, 6 x 10 = 60
12. 11, 11 x 4 = 44

Page 56
Clockwise from arrow
9 – 2, 6, 10, 8, 4, 5
4 – 10, 12, 8, 3, 7, 11
5 – 5, 11, 3, 6, 10, 9
6 – 12, 8, 10, 4, 2, 5

Page 57
1. 3 R4   5 R1   1 R2
2. 7 R1   8 R7   5 R4

Page 58
1. 22 R3   14 R5   25 R2
2. 12 R4   31 R1   19 R1

Page 59
1. .5; .7; 3.2
2. 3.5; 6.3; .1; .9; 15.4
3. 3.8
4. 12.2
5. 100.3

Page 60
1. 5/8, 2/10
2. 4/4, 1/2
3. 1, 7, 5
4. 10, 4, 7
5.
6.

Page 61
1. sleep
2. meals
3. in school
4. <, >
5. >, >
6. <, <
7.

Page 62
1. 6/7
2. 4/4
3. 8/10
4. 7/9
5. 2/4, 4/8
6. 3/4
7. 1